FROM

WINE

7 POWERFUL SCRIPTURES THAT WILL TRANSFORM YOUR LIFE FOREVER
(with Commentary, Questions and Daily Prayers)

Vincent Santiago

TABLE OF CONTENTS

INTRODUCTION

Ever since Jesus Christ performed His first miracle of transforming water into wine, billions of people across the globe have also experienced a miraculous transformation through Him. In the Bible, a transformation is defined as a renewal of a life that no longer conforms to the ways of the world in a way that pleases God (Romans 12:2).

Transformation involves those who were once far from God but drew closer to Him through the blood of Jesus Christ (Ephesians 2:13). He stands at the door of your heart and knocks. It is your job to open it to let Him in. As you experience this radical transformation on a daily basis, you may look in the mirror and find that your appearance hasn't changed much. However, those who are close to you will notice something quite different.

That transformation is Jesus Christ working in your life. It is a reflection of the nature and qualities of Christ. You might be the closest thing to God your co-workers, family or friends will ever see, and your praise is contagious. God is the source of all good things and even though He is unseen, there is something unique about a transformed life that people can't explain. You may not see God, but you can certainly see God working in people. Every hair on your head is numbered, and every cell in your body is handcrafted by the true and living God. This means that you are not only His creation, but He seeks to express Himself fully through you. This transformational process can only occur through God's miraculous power, love, grace, and mercy through His Son Jesus Christ.

Accepting Jesus Christ into your heart can transform you in ways you never thought you could. God can cleanse you from your sins of the past. He can quench old desires and the worst habits. Through repentance, faith and daily growth in Christ, He can replace all emptiness with love, hope, eternal life, fulfillment, purpose, faith, trust and all of the things the soul longs for. No longer will you be bound by chains and the dark cell that once imprisoned you. The ways of the world, it's music, gossip, attitude, desires, and values no longer become a concern. It is God that will complete you in ways further described in this transformational project.

There is great joy in the presence of the angels of God over one sinner who repents (Luke 15:10). That is a great miracle. This 7-day devotional was written for Christians as well as those curious about the faith in Jesus Christ who seek the truth, revival, wisdom, and understanding of what it means to live a transformed life. You may face trials and testings from time to time, but you can be sure that if you pick up your cross daily and stand firm in the faith in Jesus Christ, there will be no reason to fear anything. If you allow God, He can easily transform your life no matter how deep and dark your past may be.

God wants to use you in a powerful way through the gifts and talents He's given you. Today's celebrities are blessed with extraordinary gifts but seldom do they use their gifts for God. There is no doubt that their fame and fortune are rewarding, but that glory will all pass away one day. In Matthew 24:35 Jesus states that heaven and earth will pass away, but His word will last forever. He does not change with the times nor does He exist in time. He is the Alpha and Omega, the beginning and the end, and the creator of all that you see. Therefore anything that brings glory to His name will last forever, but anything else will pass away. You were designed to live a life that pleases God in everything that you do. The way you think, talk, act and participate in. You have gifts and abilities unique to anyone else in this world such as your fingerprints. You may have the gift of music, art, writing, singing or dancing. It may be the gift of patience, humor or leadership. Whatever those gifts are, God wants to bless you, elevate you and give you a deeper meaning to a life filled with purpose and joy.

Apart of the transformational process is accomplished by "being fruitful in every good work, and increasing in the knowledge of God" (Colossians 1:10). Not that our works may serve as an approval from God, but that it's become apart of our very nature to do so. The evidence of transformation is revealed in our lives as we increasingly reflect the image of Christ and His glory (2 Corinthians 3:18). A transformed life begins from the source, the power of God and the gospel message of Jesus Christ. In Acts 4:12 Peter boldly states, "Neither is there salvation in any other: for there is none other name under heaven given among men, whereby we must be saved," In John 14:6 Jesus said, "I am the way, the truth, and the life: no man cometh unto the Father, but by me." In Romans 8:9 the apostle Paul also boldly states, "But ye are not in the flesh, but in the Spirit, if so be that the Spirit of God dwell in you. Now if any man have not the Spirit of Christ, he is none of his."

When you ask God to come into your heart, He will transform you in a miraculous way. He will baptize you with His Holy Spirit and begin a great work in you. He will transform the way that you think, treat others, and the way that you treat yourself. You will also develop a deeper understanding of the way in which you view God, how He views us, and how you view yourself in this universe. You may experience some troubling times here on earth, but there is good news. It is the gospel message of Jesus Christ. The troubles of this world will never last and sunshine always follows the rain. God is infinitely more powerful and bigger than you can ever dream or imagine. How big is God? We don't know exactly, but the next time you pick up a baseball or tennis ball, think about how our universe is probably comparable in size in His hands. The most important and exciting thing is that He does, in fact, love us. No problem is too big for God to handle if you ask and trust that He will direct your path to His perfect will for your life. Whether you are suffering from confusion, hurt, lack or limitation, you can cry out to God right now because He cares. He will never leave you nor forsake you (Deuteronomy 31:6).

The Bible says in Psalms 19:1 that "the heavens declare the glory of God; and the firmament sheweth his handywork." Not only are you created in the very image of God, but He desires to have a personal relationship and wants to give you eternal life in His wonderful presence. He loved us so much that He humbled Himself from His heavenly throne and became a man, who is Jesus Christ to provide the ultimate sacrifice for the sins of mankind. The book of Genesis tells us how God created the heaven and the earth, the sun, moon, stars and every plant and animal of the land, sea, and air. He formed man from the dust of the ground in His image, breathed into his nostrils the breath of life and man became a living soul (Genesis 2:7).

Genesis 3 reveals a great separation between God and man. Our disobedience to God caused sin and death to enter into the world, and through the first man Adams sin, we all perish. Although man disobeyed God in the beginning and to this day, God provided an ultimate sacrifice to redeem man from eternal separation from Him. How significant our worth is to God if He sent His only begotten Son to take on sin and death on our behalf.

This gospel message is centered around the birth, life, death, and resurrection of Jesus Christ. Romans 3:23 tells us that all have sinned and come short of the glory of God. By understanding that the wages of sin is death (Romans 6:23), and by confessing the hopelessness of this guilt, turning from sin and placing our faith in Jesus Christ, we will receive His forgiveness and eternal life. It's a 100% free gift that we can receive through faith alone, apart from any works on our part (Ephesians 2:8-9). 1 Corinthians 15:22 says, "For as in Adam all die, even so in Christ shall all be made alive."

Perhaps you've tried to live your life according to your rules. My question to you is, what good has it brought you? I could remember as a teenager rebelling against God and His ways. I thought I knew all of the answers but I was deceived. I did not glorify Christ with the music I would listen to nor the way I thought, spoke and acted. However, God is merciful and was patiently waiting at the door of my weary heart. After coming into the knowledge of Christ and accepting Him, I immediately felt a weight lifted off my shoulders and the void in my heart was filled. Pursuing the things of the world are only temporary, but the things of God are eternal. In Romans 8:13-14 it says, "For if ye live after the flesh, ye shall die: but if ye through the Spirit do mortify the deeds of the body, ye shall live. For as many as are led by the Spirit of God, they are the sons of God." God has given you everything you need for life and godliness, and by doing the will of God you will never fall. It is a transformed life full of love, guiltless freedom and joy. One day you will receive a great welcome in the eternal kingdom by our savior Jesus Christ.

From Water to Wine introduces 7 powerful

scriptures that will help transform your life by
introducing or rekindling the flame in Christ. Take your
time as you read your daily devotional with prayers,
Biblical references, and commentary. I encourage you to
find a friend or start a small study group to study the
scriptures together discussing your thoughts, feelings or
insights amongst each other. Transformation is a process.
Day to day after increasing in the knowledge of God
through prayer and daily study of His word, you will be
transformed forever. Jesus didn't just perform the miracle
of turning water into wine right away. When His hour
came, He instructed His disciples to fill the water to the
brim and they watched Him change water into wine at a
wedding in Cana of Galilee. After His disciples witnessed
this miracle, they immediately put their faith in Him. If
you turn from a life of sin, put your faith in Jesus Christ
and believe that He rose from the grave you will have

eternal life with Christ (John 3:16). It's the best decision I've ever made in my life and it will be for you too. Not only do I sleep better at night knowing that I have eternal life, but life is satisfying in my mind, body, and soul.

Day One

Seek First The Kingdom Of God

Heavenly Father, I thank you for another day to study your word. As I prepare to hear your word today, I pray that you speak to me with clarity so that I may have a greater understanding of the true meaning of how I should live life each day. Help me to become more like you every day and provide me with the sight to see the bigger picture without fear or question. I thank you for being present each time I open up the Bible, but most of all, I'm grateful that you pulled me out of darkness. Your love is infinitely more than I can imagine. Thank you. In Jesus name, I pray. Amen.

"But seek ye first the kingdom of God, and his righteousness; and all these things shall be added unto you."

Matthew 6:33

In Matthew 6:33 Jesus gives us the answer to one of life's most difficult challenges in the Sermon on the Mount. When you seek first the things of God and His righteousness, everything from your dreams, goals, and desires will fall into place according to His will. First, seek salvation because it is the most important decision you will ever make as all of the riches in the world do not compare to the infinite riches of God. Unfortunately, it's not always that easy to trust in God's promises as we may find ourselves bound by addictions, fear or worry in attempts to fill the voids in our soul. Life can easily fall off track when we are not aligned with God's purpose and will for our lives. Therefore I pray that this study will help switch the focus back to God, His kingdom, and righteousness.

Have you ever sought after love in the wrong places? Your intentions were good but the focus was off just a bit. These things we seek after are all aspects of a relationship, such as satisfaction, happiness, and security. You may seek after money or a relationship, but they are all forms of happiness, security, and satisfaction. Seeking after material gain or status are also aspects of a relationship. Have you ever acquired any aspect of a relationship without seeking God first? How did it leave you feeling? Was it empty or a longing for something deeper? God is the only one who can fulfill every need and give us a surplus. Attaining prosperity is perfectly fine in itself, but the problem comes when we seek out these things for the sole purpose of attempting to fill something that can not be filled. There is, however, a measure of fulfillment for a season, but even King Solomon who had all the success, power, and riches in the world was still not satisfied in his soul. His downfall came when he turned his back on God by placing his will above God's. However, towards the end of his life, he states that we should fear God and keep his commandments because all of the fame and power in the world could not satisfy his soul (Ecclesiastes 12:13).

Is there modem day Solomon's today? Of course. For example, some men and women are on their 3rd and 4th marriages but fail to realize that the source of the problem is them. They are seeking something other than God to fulfill them. In this case, they are seeking for the "perfect mate" in an imperfect person. The only way to solve this problem is to accept the person God had given you and seek to be filled by the only one who can fill you. Many have said, "If I acquire that house, marriage, car or money then I'll be happy." If material possessions, status or security could create happiness, why are countless celebrities turning to destructive lifestyles in many forms? Could it be that their priorities are not in order? Eternal satisfaction, meaning, and purpose can only be filled by the true and living God. Trust in Him and He will satisfy your soul.

Today's scripture shows just one of the ways in which God works and where our focus should be. Seeking first the kingdom of God and His righteousness means that we should seek first God above everything in the world. This is because all things are temporary, but the things of God are eternal. First, we should seek salvation because it would profit you nothing if you gained the whole world and lost your own soul, even for a bit of "heaven on earth."

Does Matthew 6:33 mean that we should neglect our

daily duties that support our lives? Of course not. We are Christians who delight in the Lord because He is the source of all and He promises to add the desires of our hearts when we seek His salvation and remain obedient to Him and His will. Knowing this powerful truth will defeat worry and confusion and replace it with fulfillment and joy. You were created by the master of the universe to have a deep personal relationship so that you may glorify Him with your gifts and talents. What a great truth to know that God loves us and wants to bless us far beyond our finite minds can imagine.

Scriptures To Meditate Upon:

Matthew 6:26

Ecclesiastes 12:13

Philippians 4:19

1. What are your thoughts, feelings, and insights on the scriptures presented?

2. Are you truly seeking God first?

3. Where do you spend all of your time, money and energy?

Dear God, help me to place you above all things in this world. I know that it is so easy to lose sight of what is most important. Forgive me Father for getting caught up in the cares of this world. I ask that you will restore my vision so that my thoughts and actions all bring you glory. Thank you for your holy word, power, peace, and love. In your Son Jesus name, I pray. Amen.

Day Two

Asking God

Heavenly Father, I thank you for this opportunity to study your holy word. I pray for wisdom and understanding as I meditate upon the scriptures presented today, and that your truth may shine upon the darkness. I thank you for your grace, wisdom and infinite love. In Jesus name. Amen.

"Ask and it will be given to you; seek and you will find; knock and the door will be opened to you. For everyone who asks receives; the one who seeks finds; and to the one who knocks, the door will be opened."

Matthew 7:7-8

Matthew 7:7-8 contains two fantastic verses that can transform your life when you place God above all, as well as knowing God's will for your life. So what exactly did He mean when He said, "Ask, and it shall be given you?" This statement has often been misinterpreted by many who do not understand Jesus' verse in its proper context. At first glance, many can assume that if you ask for anything God will give it to you, but that's not what God is saying. Proponents of the word of faith movement and prosperity gospel utilized this particular verse as one of the main principles of their doctrine.

Unfortunately, many prayers continue to go unanswered and the faith of many are shattered under the assumption that if you ask God for anything, you are guaranteed 100% results with no work on your part. Is that what God teaches? The verse does say, "Ask, and it shall be given you" however further study of the scriptures indicate that God is not a genie waiting to grant any wish you have. Therefore we must read the entire chapter to gain a full understanding of what Jesus was saying in the verse.

In Matthew 7:11 Jesus states that God's will is to give His children good things if asked for. The good things God is talking about is, in fact, more of Him in the person of the Holy Spirit (Luke 11:13). Furthermore, the good things are what is best for us as we live out His will for our lives. Many do not have God's good gifts because they simply do not ask. God knows us infinitely more than we know ourselves and He will answer "yes" or "no" if it does or does not align with His will. Should we be disappointed if His answer is no, or not yet? Absolutely not. God's timing is perfect and the reality of His promise should never disappoint us. If we ask God for something we desire and He denies that request, we can be sure that it may not be the right time or it may not be good for us. He is a faithful and loving Father who is willing to say "no" to protect us. An example can be the teenager who asks his father for a shiny new sports car. Although the request may seem perfectly harmless, the reality is that it may not be the best thing for him at the moment as a father knows best for his child.

God promised us that whatever we truly need, it will always be given to us. Once God helps us develop a better understanding of what the good things are in our lives, we will always know what to ask for as we move forward with Him. John 14:15 says, "If ye love me, keep my commandments." Our obedience, love, faith and asking according to God's will, are all apart of asking in Jesus' name. The most important thing is to place God above all things, desire what God wants for us and have faith that He is looking out for our best interests. When we desire to see God's kingdom evident in our lives and in the lives of others, He is willing to give us the things we ask for according to His will. God will give you patience, mercy, grace, a heart for others and many more tools necessary to grow in Christ.

Scriptures To Meditate Upon:

Psalms 37:4

Matthew 7:11

Matthew 21:22

John 14:14-15

Luke 11:9-13

1. What are your thoughts, feelings, and insights on God's promise, love and good things God provides?

2. What are some of the things that you ask God?

Dear God, Thank you for revealing the truth about your word today. I'm grateful to serve such an awesome God who knows the things I need before I even ask. I pray for more of you Lord, more of your truth, wisdom, and understanding. Help me to understand your will for my life so that I may ask you the things that need to elevate me to new heights. I thank you for your love and grace.

In Jesus name. Amen.

Day Three

Old Things Pass Away

Dear God, as I prepare to study your word today, I pray that you will bring wisdom and revelation to my spirit. Speak to my heart and reveal your truth, love, and power. You are holy and gracious. Bless this message in Jesus name. Amen.

"Therefore if any man be in Christ, he is a new creature: old things are passed away; behold, all things are become new."

2 Corinthians 5:17

When I became a new believer in Christ years ago, I received God's Holy Spirit and became free from the weight and bondage sin had over my life. However, even as a new convert God still had some things He had to get rid of. Amongst these things was my environment, friends, self-image, and influence. We are all creatures of habit. Therefore if we are not immersed in God's word and communing with Him on a daily basis, we can easily fall back into the old self. Even though I was a new creature through Christ, I continued to have an influence that was not in conjunction with God's word. My friends, environment, as well as my own thoughts of the past, left me feeling guilty and shameful. However, one simple prayer would change my life forever. I didn't know how to pray at the time but I simply cried out to Him and He responded faster than a blink of an eye. I prayed that God will simply help me grow, to change my environment and to give me some new friends.

Within 6 months I was accepted to a biblical based

University, grew spiritually and met some amazing friends of the faith that kept a good influence. After years of attending bible study, church and listening to radio ministries in the car, I finally understood what it meant to be a new creature in Christ. I realized that I was no longer a foul-mouthed deceiving child, but I was a sinner who's past had been completely wiped clean. This meant that all of the memories of the old me was not a reflection of who I grew to be. I was a new creature bought and paid for by the grace of God. This story always serves as a reminder that when Christ died for us, our sins died with Him on the cross as well. No matter how dark your past may be, Christ will give you a new heart, mind, passion, and desire. How wonderful it is to serve such an awesome God who casts our sins into the sea of forgetfulness.

Psalms 103:12 says that He removed our transgressions as far as the east is from the west.

Therefore we must put off the old man and embrace the new life Christ has given us. Paul tells us in 2 Corinthians 14-16 that because Christ died for us, we are no longer to live for ourselves but to live for Him. Then in verse 17, he says, "Therefore if any man be in Christ, he is a new creature: old things are passed away; behold, all things are become new." As Christians, we are to live a renewed spiritual life that no longer conforms to the ways of the world. This new creature God is referring to is not a recreation of something old, nor is it an inherited nature. It is referring to a completely new creature with a new heart and a new mind.

When Christ took on the sins of this world, He lifted the weight that sin had on our lives, allowing us to become new through our faith in Him. Therefore our old nature such as pride, lust, greed, works of the flesh, bad habits, and love of sin and self all pass away when we look to Christ instead of ourselves or this world. To know that we have a second chance to experience life on a deeper level with purpose should bring a deep revelation to the professing Christian.

Once you receive this gift, the air is a bit cleaner, the food much more awesome, the Bible more meaningful and live a more interesting adventure. No longer does bitterness, hatred, greed or the things of this world affect us. Our minds have been transformed with an eternal perspective that changes the way we view God, others and ourselves. Does that mean that we have the ability to completely cease from sinning? Of course not. There is a difference between habitual sin and the natural tendency to sin.

When we begin to realize that we are a new creature in Christ, we begin to view sin as if we were looking at it through His eyes. Hating what sin is and its consequences. Unfortunately, we will all bear this burden until we enter into God's presence in heaven. We are made holy by Christ day-by-day, hating sin more and more, and turning from it not embracing it. We are no longer slaves to sin such as our former selves, but we are free from its bondage and power over us. Through Christ, we are made whole, new and alive.

Scriptures To Meditate Upon:

Romans 6:4

Romans 6:11-12

Colossians 3:9

Psalms 103:12

Ephesians 4:24

1. What are your thoughts, feelings, and insights on the scriptures presented?

Heavenly Father, thank you for filling me again with your holy and precious word. Thank you for sending your Son to take on the sins of this world to reconciling a relationship back to you. You've given me a new heart, a new mind and a new outlook on life. Give me an eternal perspective, with desires, motives, thoughts, and activities that bring glory to your name. Wipe clean my transgressions no matter how big they may seem to me. Give me more of you so that I may do your will every day. Remind me that I am no longer a slave to sin, but I am a new creature through you. Thank you. In Jesus name. Amen.

Day Four

Transformed By The Renewing Of Your Mind

Heavenly Father, I pray for wisdom and understanding as I prepare to study your word. I pray that you will bless me with a clearer picture of what it means to be transformed. I'm thankful that you are present, protecting and guiding me exactly where you want me to be. Clear away any distractions so that I may give you my full attention as I dive into your word. Shower me with your love and grace in Jesus name. Amen.

"And be not conformed to this world: but be ye transformed by the renewing of your mind, that ye may prove what is that good, and acceptable, and perfect, will of God."

Have you ever gone a day, a week or longer without being in the presence of God through prayer and study? Do you often find yourself snapping at someone easier and easier throughout the day because you didn't forgive or give it all to God? In a world full of darkness you would think we would be quick to look for the lights, but did you know that the longer we sit in darkness, the easier it is to adjust to the darkness? You'll find yourself saying things you wouldn't normally say and doing things you'd never do. And slowly but surely, we become accustomed to this new lifestyle and a new way of thinking until the light turns back on.

God is light and in Him is no darkness and the world is dark and in it is no light. The way in which the spirit of this world operates is in complete darkness, contrary to

God's light and His revelation. Therefore we must turn to the source of light on a daily basis so that we may renew our strength. Popular ideologies may seem correct, but in the end, it will only lead to death. For this reason, we must resort to godly living through our knowledge of salvation.

In the beginning of the book of Romans, Paul teaches us exactly how to live according to God's word after seeing all the great things He did for us. Because God has been so merciful to us and provided the ultimate sacrifice to save our souls, we are to present our bodies as living sacrifices, holy and acceptable to God. We no longer conform to this world but we are to be transformed by the renewing of our minds.

The good news of Christ is to receive Him through faith. Repenting from the old ways of thinking so that it develops into a new godly way of thinking. Before any action occurs, it first happens in the mind. By renewing our minds, our thoughts and action will conform to the truth of God rather than the ways of the world. How do we replace the old ways of thinking with new thoughts and actions? The answer is revealed in God's word, the Holy Bible, praise and worship, spending time with Him every day in prayer, Bible studies and through the body of Christ. Praise God for giving us strength and providing light in the darkness.

Scriptures To Meditate Upon:

1 John 1:5-9

Romans 12-16

Colossians 1:13

Ephesians 2:1-3

2 Corinthians 10:5

1. What are your thoughts, feelings, and insights on the scriptures presented?

Dear God, thank you for providing an ultimate sacrifice to save me from eternal separation from you. You are my source of life and my example to follow every day. Thank you for the gift of the Holy Spirit to lead and direct me to be more like Christ every day. Help me to be reminded to first seek you to renew my mind and my strength so that I can remain in your light. Thank you, Father, for your grace, mercy, and patience. In Jesus name. Amen.

Day Five

Trust In The Lord

Dear God, thank you for another opportunity to meditate upon your word today. I trust that you will open my eyes to a greater understanding of who you are and who I am to you. I pray that you will bless this message today and that revival takes place in my relationship with you, my thoughts and actions. In Jesus name. Amen.

"Trust in the Lord with all thine heart; and lean not unto thine own understanding."

Proverbs 3:5-6

Proverbs 3:5-6 reveals a simple truth that if we trust and follow the Lord over our plans, we will not be led astray. Isaiah 55:8-9 says, "For my thoughts are not your thoughts, neither are your ways my ways, saith the Lord." Our limited knowledge and understanding can easily lead us down a path to destruction even though it may appear to be right (Proverbs 16:25). God is omnipotent, omnipresent and omniscient, meaning that He is all powerful, all knowing, all wise and everywhere at once. He does not exist in time, therefore He will never change His standards with the time here on earth nor will He change His plan. God's plan is always perfect and we should trust in the Lord as He is the overseer of all of His creation.

Throughout history men and women have tried to bend the rules so that God may accept a new definition of right and wrong. However, when we live our lives according to what may seem right, it often leads to destruction. Think about the reign of Hitler. His plans and actions to exterminate all Jewish people seemed right in his eyes, but this only led to more terror and destruction. Not only did he wipe out countless innocent people, but think about how many generations would exist today if Hitler did not take it upon himself to essentially play God. This is just one example of many who fail to abide by God's plan.

If you've ever driven late at night, you know that your visibility is limited. There may be things going on around you that you may not see, but as you travel through the darkness, your headlights provide just enough light to keep you on course. In that same manner, God provides the light and directs your path. Although we currently live in a dark world, we can be sure that God always provides no matter how tough things may seem. You may not see the whole picture or even understand it, but as you journey with God, He will never fail you. Even the best plans created by human hands could not come close to the supreme plans that God has for you.

When you trust in God with all your heart, you are giving God the keys allowing Him to take you where He wants you to go. Will you give God the keys to elevate you to places you never thought you'd be? Or have you given God the keys but remain a backseat driver? I don't know about you but I find that to be quite annoying, especially when I know where I'm going. Or maybe you've been doing your own thing, but how is that working out for you? Following your own path will only set you up for spiritual, mental and even physical trouble. Trust in God and allow Him to take control of the wheel. Your path will always be directed in ways that our finite minds cannot perceive.

Scriptures To Meditate Upon:

1 Corinthians 13:12

Numbers 23:19

Psalms 119:142

Psalms 119:105

1. What are your thoughts, feelings, and insights on the scriptures presented?

2. Are you fully trusting in God's plan for your life?

3. Do you find yourself backseat driving most of the time?

4. What are the things in your life that you should give God control of so that he can direct a better path for you?

Heavenly Father, thank you for revealing your infinite love and power through your word today. I pray that the scriptures resonate in my heart and that I will begin applying it to my life immediately. Forgive me for following a plan that will never come close to your supreme plan. Encourage me to focus on what's most important, your plans. Lord my plans have only gone so far and you know that most have to lead to destruction and despair. Take control of the steering wheel to my life and guide my path. I trust that you will do a work in me that will exceed far beyond my imagination. Thank you.

In Jesus name. Amen.

Day Six

He Will Give Us Rest

Dear God, bless this message today and give me a more clear understanding of your word as I study today. I thank you for being present whenever I open your word and for being present every day of my life. Give me more of you God. In Jesus name. Amen.

"Come unto me, all ye that labor and are heavy laden, and I will give you rest. Take my yoke upon you, and learn of me; for I am meek and lowly in heart: and ye shall find rest unto your souls. For my yoke is easy, and my burden is light."

Matthew 11:28-30

Jesus came to earth to be put to death in order bridge the gap between God and humanity. The finished work of Christ on the cross gives us rest when we trust in Him and not ourselves. This rest is not physical. Rather, it is a spiritual rest from the heavy burden of worldly religious systems, legalism, and self-effort in order to please God or earn salvation. When you enter into God's rest, you cease to believe in your own works and believe in His finished work.

The "work" is already complete and there is no need to add or reinvent the wheel. Our job is to receive this gift through faith and allow God to produce His good fruit through us. In chapter 23 of Matthew, we read that Jesus rebukes the Pharisces for creating an unattainable system of law-keeping and self-righteous acts. When Jesus stated, "I will give you rest" in chapter 11, He was speaking to those who suffered from the heavy system of works created by the Pharisees. Hebrews 4:10 also says, "For he that is entered into his rest, he also hath ceased from his own works, as God did from his." Furthermore, God will give rest to those who trust in His promises.

I've always been intrigued by Olympic high jumpers and how they can use their momentum to jump so high. I also enjoy watching pole vaulters because they are able to clear a pole about 6 to 8 times higher. The difference between the two is one athlete is resting on something, in this case, the pole, which allows him or her to elevate to new heights. The other athlete can only go so far as they are is using their own strength to clear the pole. In that same manner, God wants us to rest in Him because He alone can forgive sin and take the burden of works, worry and guilt off our backs. He took on the heavy burden we were meant to live and through His act of obedience on the cross, we became free.

No amount of law-keeping can bring us closer to God. Jesus said that we are to take His yoke upon us and to learn from Him because His yoke is easy and the burden is light. Christ is meek and lowly in heart, and we will find rest for our souls when we come to Him. A yoke is a wooden cross piece that goes over the necks of animals in order to plow a field. When you plow a field with a heavy yoke, it can be very burdensome.

In Romans 3:20 Paul writes, "Therefore by the deeds of the law there shall no flesh be justified in his sight: for by the law is the knowledge of sin." Jesus' work on the cross took away the oppressive yoke of attempting to justify ourselves through self-righteousness. He gives us a lighter yoke to give us rest for our heavy souls when we trust Him. Which yoke are you carrying and what power are you resting on, your own or God's?

The love of God is to keep His commandments not

only for protection but the freedom which does not bear a heavy burden (1 John 5:3). Jesus' yoke is easy because His act of obedience to fulfill the law exchanged the burden we were supposed to carry. The burdens of our sins were also exchanged for His righteousness when He died on the cross. God doesn't seek to burden us with legalism, rather the Holy Spirit seeks to shape and mold us to be more like Christ through a lighter yoke lived by faith.

—

Scriptures To Meditate Upon:

Matthew 23

Romans 3:20

1 John 5:3

2 Corinthians 5:21

Hebrews 4:10

1. What are your thoughts, feelings, and insights on the scriptures presented?

2. Are you seeking to prove to God that you are faithful through good works? If so, create a list of the stressors in your life that are spiritually burdensome and give it God. There is nothing He can't handle.

Dear God, thank you for completing the work and winning the battle once and for all. I place my faith and trust fully in you. No longer will I seek to justify myself through works of the flesh, and I will allow you to complete your work through me. Take this heavy burden

off my back and I will take your yoke of faith. Help me to

learn from you. Lead and guide me. I am grateful to

experience another day in your presence. In Jesus name.

Amen.

Day Seven

God's Love For Humanity

Heavenly Father, as I prepare to study your word today, I ask that you clear any distractions that attempt to cloud my mind and to soften my heart so that I may receive your word in truth and understanding. Give me a better perspective on your love for humanity. In Jesus name. Amen.

"For God so loved the world, that he gave his only begotten Son, that whosoever believeth in him should not perish, but have everlasting life. For God sent not his Son into the world to condemn the world; but that the world through him might be saved."

John 3:16-17

John 3:16-17 is one of the greatest scriptures in the Bible. There is no greater way to summarize the gospel message than to simply let the famous verse speak for itself. Perhaps no other verse has had so much commentary. No other verse can be explained so easily. Most Bible-believing preachers will base their entire sermon on this verse. It is perhaps the most referenced verse regarding God's love for humanity.

Many consider John 3:16 to be the theme of the Bible and rightfully so. It tells us that God's love is so great that He provided His one and only Son as a sacrifice on our behalf. No other verse in the Bible so eloquently summarizes God's love for humanity and the way of salvation. That is the good news of the gospel. It's a free gift paid forward by the king of the universe and your requirement is to simply have faith in the finished work of Jesus Christ. His work on the cross paid the debt we could never pay with our own hands. He'll clear your past and give you a new life through a growing personal relationship. By choosing to follow Jesus Christ, you will be granted access to paradise.

All have sinned and fall short of God's glory, and the wages of sin is death (Romans 6:23). But God's love is so great that he took on our sin on the cross to save us from eternal separation from Him. Jesus is the way, the truth, and the life, and no name may come to the Father but through Him (John 14:6). No work of the flesh is required to be saved. This great and wonderful gift separates itself from any other faith, practice or religion. God is love and He wants to lead, guide and direct your path for a better future.

Trust and believe in God and you will see that He is in fact good. Believe in the Lord Jesus Christ and you shall be saved as stated in Acts 16:31. There is no magic formula or 12 step plan for salvation. All of the work has been completed by Christ on the cross. The only "step" is faith through God's grace. As a result of Christ being evident in your life, you will be free from the bondage of sin and you will have freedom in Christ. It is the greatest decision you'll ever make.

Scriptures to Meditate Upon:

Acts 3:19

Acts 16:31

Romans 1:16

Romans 6:23

Titus 3:5

John 14:6

1 John 1:9

Romans 5:8

Psalms 34:8

1. In your own words, summarize the essence of God's
love for humanity. What are your thoughts, feelings, and
insights on John 3:16 and the scriptures presented in
God's free gift?

Heavenly Father, thank you for the opportunity to study

your holy and precious word. I ask that you may clarify

any questions regarding your Son Jesus Christ, your

love, and salvation. I pray for wisdom and understanding

as I meditate on your word today. Fill me with your Holy

Spirit and give me the strength to live a transformed life

so that Jesus may shine through me. Thank you, Father,

for providing me with a new life through Christ and for

reaching out and saving me from eternal separation from

you. I ask that you will fill my heart with joy, peace,

hope, and love. In Jesus name. Amen.

Receiving Christ As Your Savior

We've all sinned and come short of God's glory. If you'd like to receive Christ as your Lord and savior or re-dedicate your life to Him, remember that there are no "steps" to salvation. There is also no required work to perform to earn your way into heaven.

The work has already been completed on the cross. The only requirement is to have faith in the finished work that Christ has done. He covered the sins of this world with His precious blood to saves us from eternal separation. Believe in your heart that He died, was buried and rose again 3 days later to reconcile the relationship between God and humanity.

Allow Christ to come into your heart by believing and following Him and you will be with Him for eternity after you pass. Understand that you are not saved because of a prayer you prayed once before or even today. You are saved by grace through faith when you ask Christ to come into your heart, believe in His finished work and repent from sin. He will give you a new life and bring you to new heights. He will never leave you or forsake you. He will lead and direct you to places you never thought you'd be. Pray and read your word every day. He is the source of strength. Find a Bible-believing church and friends of faith so that you may hold each other accountable.

Dear Jesus Christ, I've tried everything, but at the end of the day, there was always a void in my heart. I've been longing for meaning and purpose and I've been trying to fill it with everything but you. I have sinned and come short of your glory. I believe in your finished work on the cross and want to have a personal relationship with you.

I believe that you died on the cross, was buried and rose

again to save me from eternal separation from you. You

took the burdens and cares of this world off my back so

that I can walk in freedom and victory. Forgive me of all

of my sins and give me a fresh start with you. I believe in

you alone, and no amount of self-righteous acts or

religion will save me. I thank you for the free gift of

salvation and for reconciliation. Thank you for your rich

love, mercy, and grace. In Jesus name. Amen.

Scriptures To Meditate Upon:

John 3:16

John 1:12

John 14:6

Matthew 28:19-20

Ephesians 2:8

Ephesians 2:13

Ephesians 6:10-18

Isaiah 40:31

DISCLAIMER & TERMS OF USE AGREEMENT

opinions and not professional advice. Vincent Santiago

makes no guarantee or promise as to any results that may

be obtained from using the information provided. You are

solely responsible for the use of any content and hold

Vincent Santiago harmless in any event or claim.

Manufactured by Amazon.ca
Bolton, ON

23866962R00039